Love's Sweet Music

Adam McKim

"Love lifts us up where we belong."
— Christian

Love Hanging By A Thread

I'm not yet in love,
For it is hanging by a thread,
But soon it will break,
And my love, it will shed.

With it broken, I will fall
Until I hit the ground.
Only then will I be running —
Destination… lovebound.

I hope she understands
My feelings for her.
Will she accept them?
I know not for sure.

But there it is, hanging
By a thread so thin,
Hiding in the dark —
So secret and dim.

Waiting to be unlocked
From my heart with a key.
Only then will my love
Be released and set free.

Until then I dream of her
As I lie there in my bed,
Waiting for the break —
Of love hanging by a thread.

Forever With You

Our journey was started years ago,
Alone we walked in time so slow.
Filled with heartbreak, our memories past —
The future is now with us at last.

Together we walk, no longer alone,
Forming paved roads from stepping stones.
Overcoming sadness from time before,
Together we walk through a new door.

Keep me in your heart, as I will for you.
Our love is strong, pure, and true.
We cannot deny this passion we found —
Our love is connected, tied, and bound.

I will love you forever, as you will love me.
My heart was locked up, but you had the key,
And yours I unlocked with a key of my own.
Together our love was released and shown.

Forever will we love, forever will we fly,
Forever will we have this love of you and I.
Forever will we laugh, forever will we cry,
Forever will we walk together side by side.

In The Stillness Of The Night

In the stillness of the night,
A faint cry for love is heard,
Echoing far into the distance,
Soaring higher than any bird.

In the stillness of the night,
Under the moonlight shining,
She hears his painful cry
While alone she is dining.

She starts on a journey
To seek out his heartfelt cry,
For if she ignores his plea,
A new love may pass her by.

In the stillness of the night,
As she wanders on her way,
She must find this lost soul —
She cannot turn away.

For she is lost as well;
Deep inside, she also weeps.
Though she may not know it,
He also wanders as he seeks.

His cry for love gets louder,
Her cry as well echoes out.
In the stillness of the night,
Together they wander about.

As they draw ever closer,
Their loneliness begins to fade,
For their journey is coming to an end —
From this love that has conveyed.

They come together at last,
Under the midnight sun.
In the stillness of the night,
Two young lovers have begun.

A Poet To Be

A poet I claim not to be,
For words are never there.
In all the years I've tried to write,
I have no words to share.

I sit and think, but nothing comes —
No inspiration here.
I want to write of anything,
But still no words, I fear.

I read the works of other poets;
I wish I were like them.
How do they write such beautiful lines?
A poet — I'm not him.

I try to write from the heart,
From deep within my soul.
I try to write of the love I have,
But cannot reach my goal.

But why, I ask, why can't I write
Of love so pure and true?
Why can't I write about her eyes —
A mix of green and blue?

I want to write about her smile;
It brightens up my day.
I try to think of anything,
But words I cannot say.

I wish I knew how to write
A poem with such bliss.
I wish I knew how to describe
Her soft but tender kiss.

I cannot even begin to write
How she holds me tight —
How her arms around me
Make everything just right.

A poet does not have to think;
The words flow right out.
When I sit and try to write,
I want to scream and shout.

I mean, come on, how hard can it be
To write about her hair?
Such long, beautiful, natural blonde
That flows in the air.

I try to write about her laugh —
The words will not fly.
Time passes, and finally,
I say it's soft and high.

It's been an hour and a half;
I'm stuck on verse twelve.
I cannot find a rhyme to use —
I go online and delve.

A poet does not do that,
Go online to find a rhyme.
A poet has it in his head
And can write at any time.

But a poet I am not,
For I cannot write of love —
How the girl I am with
Is an angel from up above.

How I love her with all my heart
And want to spend my life with her.
How her love for me is more
Than I can ever be, for sure.

As I draw near the end,
My mind is not so numb.
I realize I've just written of love —
A poet I have become.

When You Wake

When you wake, think of me —
You're in my thoughts as well.
Put a smile upon your face,
For in your heart I dwell.

Lie there a moment, don't you move,
Don't even blink an eye.
Imagine I am there with you —
Your sweet and loving guy.

Hold me in your arms so tight,
Don't ever let me go.
Tell me that you love me
More than I will ever know.

I wake myself and do the same —
Imagine you're here too.
Before our day has begun,
There's only me and you.

A New Feeling

A new feeling has arisen —
What could it be?
A new emotion of the heart,
Someone new for me?

What is this feeling that I feel,
This thing I have inside?
Could it be I found new love —
Someone new I can confide?

The pain I had is fading now;
Joy takes its place.
The memories of the past,
Taken over by a new face.

A new path I have chosen
To walk from now on.
The darkness has gone away —
I wake up to a new dawn.

A Love Like Hers

A love like hers
Flows within my heart,
Makes me feel young again —
A new, fresh start.

A love like hers,
So tender and sweet.
A single kiss from her lips
Makes my heart skip a beat.

It's hard to explain
Her love for me,
But easy to feel
And obvious to see.

How her love is real,
Forever living,
Will always be there —
Forever giving.

Just A Love Poem

Your amazing eyes, your beautiful smile,
Take my breath away for a while.
I catch it again, give you a kiss.
To be yours forever is my wish.

A breeze in the night, your hair in the wind,
The windows down as we round the bend.
Wherever we go, whatever we do —
Just as long as I'm with you.

Holding you tight as we sleep,
Still together in dreams so deep.
Seeing you wake in the morning sun,
Still holding each other in our arms as one.

Still lost in the warmth of your gentle touch,
Holding you close means so very much.
I love you so much and always will.
'Til the end of time, I'll love you still.

I Miss You

As I lie here by myself,
A tear comes to my eye.
It's been a while since I saw you,
And time will not fly.

I miss you very much —
The distance is too great.
But I know you are mine;
I won't deny our fate.

But still, I want you in my arms,
I want you by my side.
I miss the way you hold me,
When in you I would confide.

Everything about you,
Everything you do.
Every time I'm here alone —
Baby, I miss you.

Our First Date
(Tri-Fall)

The silence around us,
As we see
The stars shooting across the skies...
From this beautiful dust
Above me,
The stars reflect into your eyes.

The moonlight shines on you
In this night,
Bringing out your amazing smile...
And when the morning dew
Comes in sight,
Our night together was worthwhile.

This night was our first date —
Only us.
I'll never forget holding you...
And as we accept fate
With a buss,
The start of new love as sparks flew.

I Promise You
(Trijan Refrain)

Oh love of mine, oh love of mine,
Come to me in this day.
I'll save you from this world's opine —
These judgments I will slay.
I'll hold you in my arms so tight
And shield our love with all my might...
I promise you
I promise you
Oh love of mine, I'll always fight.

Oh love of mine, oh love of mine,
I'll always keep you warm.
Through thick and thin, it will be fine —
I'll shield you from the storm.
Through all the battles and the wars,
No matter their rank or their scores...
I promise you
I promise you
To keep love strong — what's mine and yours.

Oh love of mine, oh love of mine,
I'll fight this to the end.
I'll put myself on the front line
To be there to defend.
I'll never let them take our love —
This gift was given from above...
I promise you
I promise you
Our love they'll never deprive of.

If She Be The One

I pray to Thee, Lord,
If she be the one,
Then all I ask
Is let it be done.

I pray to Thee, Lord,
If this be our fate,
Then guide me to her —
Don't make me wait.

I pray to Thee, Lord,
My one God above,
Show me what it's like
To have true love.

I pray to Thee, Lord,
Please do not shun.
Let love take a chance,
If she be the one.

True Love At Last

Everything in the past,
The memories pushed away —
All for one final love,
No more heartbreaks, I pray.

You have shown me true love,
What it's really about.
You gave me your heart,
Which holds no doubt.

My past was filled with sadness,
Never knowing if I'll find love.
But then you came along —
A true gift from God above.

That gift was true love —
True love at last.
Our future will be forever,
And our future is vast.

Love's Embrace

Filled with happiness when I'm with you,
There are no days that are sad and blue.
No doubt that you take me to a better place,
And wrap me tight in your love's embrace.

Your smile is filled with warmness, I see,
Your laughter says you are happy with me.
Your heart is as soft as velvet and lace,
Still pulling me into your love's embrace.

Gone are the days I searched high and low,
Taking every hit of heartbreak's mighty blow.
No longer do I feel the pain of tears down my face —
You wiped them all away with your love's embrace.

Now here I stand to return that love to you,
My heart will always be yours, faithful and true.
We both found true love, wrapped in God's grace,
To each other we are wrapped, in our love's embrace.

A Dream Come True

I dream of a life where I'm happy and free,
A life with someone who's happy with me.
I dream of a love, a passion-filled heart,
Between two souls that will never part.

I dream of a smile that never fades;
Through darkest times, it shines through the shades.
I dream of a laughter in a pure, simple bliss —
I dream of all the days I never want to miss.

I dream of eternity with my special one,
A dream come true, for it's already begun.
When you came along, that's when I knew
That I would be living all my dreams with you.

A Distant Hope

A distant hope
Miles beyond reach,
But nothing that two hearts
Can't easily breach.

A distant hope
May seem out of control,
But love has a way
Of fulfilling its goal.

A distant hope
May seem like a dream,
But dreams can come true
With two hearts as a team.

A distant hope
May be distant now,
But time and patience
Will close distance somehow.

My Angel Love
(Trijan Refrain)

My angel love, my angel love,
Such beauty in my eyes,
You're sent to me from God above,
For Heaven heard my cries.
He sent you with a love so pure,
A divine soul that's sure to cure...
My broken heart
My broken heart
Is safe within your wings, secure.

My angel love, my angel love,
You take away the chains.
You help me break away free of
The heartaches and the pains.
You wrap me up and hold me tight
And pull me out into the light...
We fly away
We fly away
My angel love, this feels so right.

My angel love, my angel love,
Don't ever let me go.
I give my thanks to God above
For sending you below.
And when our time comes to an end,
From all the years which we transcend...
I'll follow you
I'll follow you
To Heaven we will both ascend.

I Sing A Song

I sing a song of a thousand words,
A love song just for you.
It flows within my heart and soul —
Will you sing it too?

Join me in this lovely song,
Sing it with me, dear.
Shout it out from deep within,
For everyone to hear.

I sing a song of a thousand words,
A song so filled with love —
A song that also birds will sing,
Even the mourning dove.

We'll sing it all the time, my love,
Throughout every day —
This love song of a thousand words,
For each other we convey.

Connected By Stars

As I look up at the stars,
Shining bright in the night skies,
I know somewhere out there
They are seen by your eyes.

A reflection of you
sparkles from the dust —
A hope that someday
they'll shine on us.

Connected by stars
under moonlight,
Trading reflections
throughout each night.

Love's Sweet Music

As our heartbeats collide,
The emotion of passions confide.
The rhythm of the night so soft and slow,
As the music of love gently flows.

Don't Let Me Go

A distant hope connected by stars,
Somehow lost in time.
Slowly brewing up again,
Aged like fine wine.

Time was lost but feelings not —
They were always there.
Staying on each other's mind,
Our hearts always cared.

As days went on in our lives,
Paving our own ways,
Sometimes crossing each other's paths
Throughout this hectic maze.

Now here we are once again —
We should let this grow.
Here's my heart, give me yours...
Please don't let me go.

Come With Me

Come with me,
and I'll take you to a place called home,
Where love is the foundation that is built on trust.

Come with me,
and I'll protect you with the security of my arms,
Where holding you is all you need to feel safe.

Come with me,
and I'll humor you with laughter and joy,
Where high-spirited words are all you need to feel happy.

Come with me,
and you'll feel a love so divine,
Where forever I'm yours, and forever you're mine.

No Other But You

The distance takes a lonely toll,
For you are far away.
But every night I dream of you,
And smile every day.

Even though you're way out there,
I keep you on my mind.
For a distant hope is all I have,
Which someday will decline.

Until then, I'll be right here —
I promise to stay true.
My heart is locked 'til you are here;
There is no other but you.

Temptations

We finally meet beneath the stars,
After many long nights alone.
Your eyes sparkle with the reflections
of the galaxy above.

We kiss under the moonlight,
Your lips softly caress mine.
Your hair sweeps across my face,
Sending tingles throughout my body.

We lay on the sandy beaches,
As temptations begin to rise.
The waters engulf the fiery flames,
The waves cool the heat of passion.

Our hearts race and our souls yearn,
To embrace and become one.
We hold each other, temptations resisted,
We surrender to the moment instead.

Take Me Home

They say home is where the heart is —
It doesn't have to be a place.
Your love is the house
Where I long to be embraced.

If you invite me in,
I'll forever stay by your side.
Take me home to your love,
Where forever I will reside.

The Heart Of Death

It was a night like any other as I drove myself to work,
Winding through the snowy roads where Death likes to lurk.
As my tires swam through slush and the winds picked up speed,
Death hid in the banks, working up his dirty deed.

Then across the snowy median of I-86,
I saw a car fishtail toward me as it glided on the slick.
For a second I was as frozen as the ice on my breath,
And right there, stood before me, was the one and only Death.

"I have come for you tonight, for this death is your fate.
Don't try to plead for your life, for I will not wait."
He reached out for me with his grimly hand.
"Wait," I said with a smile, "let me change your plan."

Death drew back his hand as he looked at me in shock,
For no other had the guts to challenge his death clock.
"What can you say to me to make me change my mind?"
He said with a laugh, "I do not have the time."

I knew if I showed Death what lies deep within my heart,
He would know it's not yet time for life and I to part.
As we stood on the highway, beneath the frozen storm above,
I whispered unto Death, "Do you believe in love?"

"I do not know of love… only pain, despair, and dread,"
Said Death as he slowly began to bow his head.
I could see I got his attention, so I continued on.
I told him of a story that would last until the dawn.

"Death, I know you want to take me to the Angels in the sky.
God already sent me one, but this one does not fly.
She walks upon the earth; she is of heart and soul.
She breathes the breath of life — of which many you have stole."

"I cannot change fate," he said. "I cannot spare your breath."
"But you can," I corrected. "You are the Angel of Life and Death."
"Tell me," he said with a smirk, "why should I spare your life?"
"Because..." I said with a tear, "she has yet to be my wife."

Death took a step back as he looked me in the eyes.
We stood in silence for a moment beneath the frozen skies.
He then walked toward me as he looked me up and down.
An inch from my broken face, he asked with a frown:

"Where is this angel you speak of, in which you claim to be in love,
The one you say God sent you from the heavens up above?
I've never seen her in your life. I've never seen her around.
Tell me now why I shouldn't, in this moment, strike you down."

"I have yet to meet her, for I love her from afar."
I then said with a smile, "We are connected by the stars.
I have still yet to hold her in my loving arms.
I have yet to caress her heart with all my loving charms.

I have yet to share a kiss with her soft, tender lips.
I have yet to dance with her, with my arms around her hips.
Death, if you spare me from an end in this cold,
You can come for us both when we live life and grow old."

Death pulled off his hood, and from his hollow eyes,
Tears streamed down his skull as he began to cry.
Then across the snowy median of I-86,
I saw a car drive on by into the snowy winter mix.

A Day Without You

A day without you
is like a fish without the sea.
It's as dry as the leaves
falling from the autumn tree.

A day without you
is like a bee without the flower —
No honey for the bears
to seek out and devour.

It is a part of nature
for these things to be together.
Separating them is like
the sky without the weather.

A day without you
is like a heart without the soul,
For it is in our nature
to be together as a whole.

Please Take My Heart
(Trijan Refrain)

I long for you, I long for you,
To hold me in your arms.
I long for you to love me now
And win me with your charms.
I wish to be your one true love,
To be your blessing from above...
Please take my heart
Please take my heart
Our love God's sure to be proud of.

I long for you, I long for you,
To need me in your heart.
I wish to be the brushstrokes of
Your lovely work of art.
Please paint me in your life today —
The colors your love will convey...
Please take my heart
Please take my heart
And paint it what your love portrays.

I long for you, I long for you,
To keep me in your thoughts.
I hope to someday be the one
You wish to tie the knot.
I wish for you to need me now;
I hope you will someday, somehow...
Please take my heart
Please take my heart
I hope to someday make those vows.

Road Of Love

We have started on a journey,
Of love we can't deny.
Paving every step of the way,
This road for you and I.

There are no stops on this road,
There is no time to rest.
We take our love all the way,
We do our very best.

If there is an end in sight,
It will be Heaven's door.
There we'll keep on paving,
This road of love forevermore.

If I Could Be

If I could be your sweetest kiss,
I'd fill it with the purest bliss.
If I could be your biggest hug,
I'd make you feel all nice and snug.

If I could be your greatest smile,
I would make them all worthwhile.
I would make your heart sing,
If I could be your everything.

Love's Inferno

A single touch sparks
a fire in our eyes,
A flame of passion slowly rising
from the depths of our souls.
Casting our shadows on the wall,
dancing in a blaze of luminosity.

In a heat of desire,
we embrace in a sea of flames,
Our souls scintillating
under the rising inferno,
Our hearts ferociously beating in sync,
reverberating over the crackling embers.

Kindling our spirits
with immensities of amorousness.
An explosion of culmination
sings out in rhapsody,
As we envelop and relinquish
to love's inferno.

Through The Storm

The skies in my world were darkened
by the nightmares of my heartbreaks,
Rendering me blind, sending me
wandering, lost off the path of love.

Thundering cries of pain echoed
from the depths of my soul,
Striking me at the core of my heart,
shattering it into a million pieces.

The dark clouds stopped at nothing
to follow my every step,
Surrounding me with a wall of thickness,
unable to breathe.

Raining down on me
heavy tears of sorrow,
Soaking me to the bone
with painful memories of the past.

Then a flicker of light caught my eye,
and there you were,
A beautiful angel descending
from the heavens above.

You embraced me with your loving arms,
wrapping me in your wings,
Shielding me from the painful strikes,
easing my cries of anguish.

With every smile, you picked up
the pieces of my broken heart,
And with the most delicate hands of comfort,
you mended it back together.

Guiding me back to the path of love,
no longer lost in darkness,
You helped me through the storm —
and for that, I love you.

A Paradelle Of Us
(The Paradelle)

Passionately penning of our love for one another,
Passionately penning of our love for one another.
Scripting our dreams from above with grace,
Scripting our dreams from above with grace.
With dreams for one another… penning of our love,
Passionately scripting our grace from above.

From deep within our hearts, we write of us,
From deep within our hearts, we write of us.
Giving parts of our souls to each — you and me,
Giving parts of our souls to each — you and me.
We write from deep within, giving our parts
To each of us… you and me… souls of our hearts.

In the end we are together… living our story,
In the end we are together… living our story.
We perfectly blend in every word,
We perfectly blend in every word.
Living every word in our story… we blend,
We are perfectly together in the end.

We passionately write from deep within our hearts,
Dreams of one another… penning in our parts,
Scripting for our story with grace from above,
Giving to each of us every word of our love.
We are living together in the end —
You and me… our souls... we perfectly blend.

Heartbeats On My Mind

I love you.
It's as simple as that.
Every thought of you is a heartbeat.
My heart is racing.
You are forever on my mind,
For I'd die without you.

My Heart Is An Open Book

My love is scripted in my heart.
I open it up to you like a book.

Read it every day and you will see,
My love for you grows with every chapter.

My World

You are the light in my eyes for guiding me,
The waters that nourish the stem of my soul,

The trees that sway toward me in your gentle breeze,
As I am embraced by the branches of your love.

If I had enough time to list them all, I would —
But for now, you are the world to me.

Love Invitation

The look in our eyes invites us to love each other,
A longing to be filled with the desires of our hearts,
Our fingers gently feathering up and down our bodies,
As the tingles send shock waves of emotions through us.

We embrace each other as we fall into a passionate kiss,
Your lips caressing mine, the sweet smell of your hair.
As I pull your head back and I gently kiss your neck,
You gasp with pleasure while pulling me closer.

The temptation is too much, and we rip off our clothes,
Tossing them aside as we gaze upon each other.
Another kiss sets the motion, and we become one,
Dancing to the beat of our hearts colliding in sync.

The sheets tangle around our bodies, binding us together,
Tossing and turning as we balance our rhythm,
As if we were lost at sea, rocking in a raging storm —
We gaze into each other's eyes, never once looking away.

A bite on the lips sends a jolt through your body,
Convulsing as you cling on with all of your strength.
We fall back on the bed as we are breathless and weak,
From the passions of our sensual love invitation.

My Love For You

I love you like the sun loves to shine,
Shedding light within your life,
Beaming rays of heat within your soul —
My love is the warmth upon your heart.

I love you like lightning loves to strike,
Sending shock waves within your body,
Coursing throughout you with steady flow —
My love is the current on which your emotions ride.

I love you like oxygen loves to give existence,
Filling the emptiness in your lungs,
Desiring to live each and every day —
My love is your breath of life.

There are many other ways that I love you so.
I have drained my heart and soul.
I am empty inside, so I ask you now:
Will you love me like I love you?

As A Poet

As a poet, I must write
Of my one and only love.
I'll not conceal my desire
To share my gift from above.

As a poet, I must praise her,
Write of her beauty and her grace.
I must share my inner feelings
When I look upon her face.

As a poet, I must love her,
If indeed that it is true.
My love started as a seed —
As I wrote for her, it grew.

As a poet, I must be there
To give her words of hope.
I'll write a rope of loving words
To help pull her up the slope.

As a poet, I must not hide —
My heart is an open book.
For anytime she needs my love,
She is welcome for a look.

As a poet, I must not hate.
I'll not write poison on the heart,
For it is scripted with a pain
That would tear us both apart.

As a poet, I must not lie —
Her trust I never will betray.
I'll write in words of honesty —
It's true love I will convey.

As a poet, I must not greed.
I'm only hers if she desired.
I'll only write of generosity —
Her love will never be required.

As a poet, I must not lust,
For it's her love I wish to wed.
I'll write of holy matrimony
To take place before the bed.

As a poet, I will conclude
That for her, I'll always write —
To be in her thoughts every day,
And in her dreams every night.

Forever Us

You hear that, my love?
It's my heart — it sings.
Listen, my love,
Listen to the strings.

It sings of my passion,
So raw with the solo.
An acoustic of melodies —
Oh… listen to it flow.

My love, do you hear?
It sings a song thus.
It's a song of our love —
I call it Forever Us.

If Only

If only I could hold you in my arms right now,
Embrace you with my love so true and divine,
Wrap you up with the emotions of my heart —
I'd make you feel at home within my soul.

If only I could look deeply into your brown eyes
As I tell you how much I love you so.
I would caress your face with my gentle hand;
I'd kiss away your pain, make you forget your worries.

If only I could just be there for you right now,
Instead of you being alone, lost, and confused.
I would make you feel like the luckiest girl
To have my love so pure within your heart.

Let Me Be Your Everything

You know everything that you are to me.
You're my special angel — you'll always be.
Let me take this time to tell you now
What I want to be to you — I'll tell you how.

I want to be your rock when you're sinking low.
I want to be your smile that really makes you glow.
I want to be your heaven when you feel you're in hell.
I want to be the door that opens up your shell.

I want to be everything you are to me.
Your heart is locked — let me be the key.
You're my special angel, my right hand.
Please let me be your special man.

A Vision Of Us

We are alone, but not for long.
With each other is where we belong.
Someday soon we will meet —
Broken hearts will be complete.

When that day comes and some time,
Bells ring out their wedding chime.
I push back your veil of lace —
We say "I do," and then embrace.

Children's laughter as they play,
The miracles of everyday.
Faith in God to hold our bond —
Here on earth and far beyond.

Our children grow and we are old,
As our dreams had foretold.
This is my vision of our life —
I vision us husband and wife.

A Letter To My Love

As I sit here, I can't help but smile at the thought of you.
I think about everything I have written, the old and new.
I write of my love for you, but I want to make sure you know —
These words that I write are true to my heart, not just show.

In reality, there are no words that can truly express the love inside,
Even if I wrote a trail of words that could stretch worldwide.
But it's all I can do to show my love when you live far away,
But know in your heart that I mean every word every day.

You know that I love you with all of my heart and soul.
I never want you to doubt that my love isn't whole.
Just keep in mind, my dear, when you're ready to decide —
My love for you in words will be the same as by your side.

I Wait For An Angel

An angel walks among the earth,
One who I adore with all my heart.
With brown hair and deep brown eyes,
A passion for penning works of art.

I am in love with this angel —
She is the one I know for me.
I'll wait as long as it takes;
For her, I will always live free.

I will always be here for her,
Whenever she needs a friend.
I'll still hang on to my dreams
Of being with her in the end.

An angel walks among the earth.
I'll love her 'til the end of days.
For my heart will stay true to her —
I hope that someday she repays.

Falling In Love From Afar

Love… to me,
is meeting someone you have never met.
You talk about hopes, dreams,
and what you want in life.

You both take everything in
and never once forget —
Already you feel
she'd be the perfect wife.

Though you still haven't met her,
you feel the love.
I know it may sound crazy,
maybe even bizarre.

Love… to me,
is meeting your angel sent from above,
but must get to know her heart
and fall in love from afar.

Love Across the Sea

Beauty engulfs the screen as I see her for the first time.
My heart jumps as she waves — the rhythm begins to climb.
She wears a black dress, long dark hair and eyes.
I knew from that moment where my love truly lies.

She steals my heart with her gorgeous smiles.
We talk as if she's here, though she's many miles.
A new life has begun on opposite sides,
Keeping in touch while the ocean divides.

A month down the road, vacation is planned,
For I must follow my heart to another land.
I count down the days to when I reach the clouds.
Soon I will be walking in unknown crowds.

Thirty thousand feet, twenty-four hours —
I am on my way, the distance I devour.
I land in Manila, stepping out into the heat.
All eyes are upon me, no time to retreat.

I look around as I stand there, all alone at the gate,
Surrounded by a language I cannot translate.
An hour goes by — my signal is weak.
Somewhere close by, it's me she seeks.

Then there she was, running in my direction —
My beautiful island girl in such perfection.
We embrace in our arms with tears of joy —
The Filipina girl, the American boy.

Two weeks with her, our love only grows.
I'm back at home — the pain, it shows.
Our love has just begun, but now we must wait.
We'll be together again — we will soon seal our fate.

A Lovely Name

Her lovely smile,
Her lovely eyes,
Her lovely hair —
Dark as night skies.

I can't get enough
Of her lovely heart.
I'm with her always,
Though we're far apart.

A lovely call,
A lovely talk —
If only the distance
Was a lovely walk.

The most lovely thing
About her is the same:
Her name is Lovely —
A lovely name.

A November Wedding

A November day, cold and bitter,
The leaves lay fallen on the ground.
The skies are cloudy with chance of rain,
No sound in the air, silence surround.

Dim and gloomy, the day looks dead,
For the colors of life have faded.
The sun has hidden its rays of warmth,
For summer has made it jaded.

Then silence is broken with words of new life,
Warm embrace of our hands as if gloved.
Smiles paint the colors of life on this day,
With two words spoken: "Dearly beloved."

We are gathered here today to witness our love,
To celebrate the joining of two hearts.
A cold, bitter day now warm with passion —
Today we wed... 'til death do us part.

Adam & Lovely
November 25, 2016

About the author:

Adam McKim was born and raised in a small town in Missouri, where he still lives today with his wife and son. He began writing in his early twenties and has authored a growing collection of poems and books. When he's not writing, he enjoys quiet moments with family and the continued pursuit of storytelling.